NATURE'S CATHEDRAL

A CELEBRATION OF THE
NATURAL HISTORY MUSEUM BUILDING

PUBLISHED BY THE NATURAL HISTORY MUSEUM, LONDON

INTRODUCTION

IT IS 1873, THE VICTORIAN era is in full stride and in South Kensington the foundation stone of a new museum has just been laid. Conceived as the new home of the greatest and most extensive natural history collection ever assembled, it is also designed to reflect the confidence, energy and scientific drive of the age. The building will become the Natural History Museum and the architect is Alfred Waterhouse.

The new Museum's parent institute was the British Museum, which had been founded in 1753 when the personal collections of Sir Hans Sloane were bought by the nation on his death. They contained a multitude of items including books and manuscripts, coins, works of art and other objects, particularly those connected with natural history. There were all manner of specimens large and small, from mollusc shells and bird skins to skeletons and horned skulls, insects and dried plants. They came from all over the world but particularly from territories forming the British Empire and those countries with which Britain had strong trading connections, such as China and the USA. At the time of Sloane's death, the collections filled two houses. They were purchased for the nation using funds raised by the first ever national lottery and were installed first

A watercolour of one of the galleries painted in 1888, seven years after the Museum opened.

in Montague House and later in the current British Museum building in Bloomsbury. Initially, at least, additions to the new national collections showed little in the way of any underlying plan. Rather, donations were accepted in a haphazard fashion, the only criterion being that the material was of 'museum quality'. Change came with the realisation that in order to obtain as complete a coverage as possible, a more systematic approach to sourcing specimens was needed.

The 18th century had been the Age of Enlightenment for science, with a burgeoning curiosity in how the natural world worked and the elucidation of many scientific principles. The 19th century saw a greater emphasis on describing the natural world. By the 1860s there was a new appreciation of the variety of life found on the planet and of the relationships of species to each other, not least through Darwin's recently published and (then) very controversial theory on the origin of species. Descriptive taxonomy – the identification, naming and description of species – and the placement of organisms into classifications based on their similarity and presumed relationships to each other, would be a driving force for the next hundred years, and continues today. Assessing the full range of variation in any species of plant or animal requires examination of many examples of that organism, and the vast collections of the British Museum were ideally suited to the task. However, by the middle of the century, the collections had grown to the point where the building was so full that new specimens were being turned away. After extensive debate, some of it sharp to the point of vitriolic, the decision was made to remove all the natural history collections to a separate site. The location selected for the new building was South Kensington.

South Kensington had been marked as a potential centre for science and the arts following the success of the Great Exhibition, held in Hyde Park in 1851. Indeed, with the enthusiastic support of Prince Albert, much of the land and properties in South Kensington had been gradually purchased

Richard Owen (1804–1892), the first Director of the Museum, at the age of 40. He famously identified the extinct giant moa from only a fragment of leg bone, which he is seen holding in this portrait.

to provide a site for institutes to continue the aims of the Great Exhibition and 'extend the influence of Science and Art upon Productive Industry'. The area already contained the South Kensington Museum itself (renamed by Queen Victoria in 1899 as the Victoria & Albert Museum) and there were plans to build others. More importantly, it offered a large site, an advantage not lost on the new Museum's first Superintendent, Richard Owen. During the seemingly interminable arguments on the merits of choosing South Kensington over smaller but more central sites he had proclaimed: 'while I love Bloomsbury, I love ten acres more'. The generosity of space would allow Owen to advance his own ideas for a great, modern museum in which the public would marvel at the wonders of Creation. It would be a veritable cathedral to nature. Eventually the arguments and counter-arguments passed. In 1864 a site in the relatively rural suburb of South Kensington was confirmed and Owen was given the go-ahead.

In 1862 the site of the modern Natural History Museum was occupied by 'one of the ugliest public buildings ever raised in this country', which had been used that year for an international exhibition. To the north of it lay extensive gardens belonging to the Royal Horticultural Society. One year later, the site was purchased by the Government and the exhibition building demolished to provide a 12 acre (4.86 hectare) open site for the new Museum. At the same time (January 1864), an architectural competition was held with a first prize of £400 for a design incorporating the new Natural History Museum, a Patents Museum and several other, unspecified museums.

This proved to be a false start, as the original winner of the architectural competition, Captain Francis Fowke (ironically the same man who designed the ugly building that the Museum was to replace), died almost immediately! In 1866 Alfred Waterhouse, a young architect from the north of England, was appointed to translate the winning design into reality but a change of government from Liberal to Conservative delayed the project for a further 18 months. When it restarted, most of the winning design had gone, swept away along with the Patents and other museums. Although the Natural History Museum survived, the final building would bear only traces of the original winning design.

Alfred Waterhouse was a Quaker, born in Liverpool in 1830 to wealthy, mill-owning parents. An aspiring and talented artist, he turned to architecture as a profession and spent a year travelling and studying in Europe, especially in France, Germany and Italy, where the ecclesiastical architecture made a particular impression on him. He was also strongly influenced by the great names of the day such as Ruskin, Pugin and Scott. Returning to England, he set up a practice in Manchester, rapidly made a name for himself and moved to London. Eventually, he became renowned as an expert in Gothic style and one of, if not the, most financially successful Victorian architects. Waterhouse was more than an architect in the modern sense of the word. His wide interests, obsession with detail and belief in the importance of decoration made him a combination of architect, structural engineer and interior designer.

Waterhouse had not even entered the original competition for the new Museum and, while he had previously designed a variety of buildings including Manchester Assize Courts (now sadly demolished), he had never been involved with anything on this scale. His brief was to provide a building offering sufficient space to store the vast collections, facilities for the research staff, and two types of gallery: one to display example specimens suitable as an introduction for lay

Alfred Waterhouse was only 36 when he was offered the chance to build the new museum in South Kensington. The project occupied the next 14 years of his life.

people and another for those with more detailed knowledge of the subject, all in a magnificent setting and to a very tight budget. He had also to take into account practicalities such as moving large specimens into and around the Museum, maintaining the internal environment of a large building, and even future technological advances – illuminating the galleries by gaslight was one possibility under consideration.

At the end of 1868, with work about to start in South Kensington, the whole project was put up in the air again when a new Commissioner of Works suggested that it might be better to use a site on the Embankment, opposite what is now the Royal Festival Hall. A Parliamentary Select Committee was set up to look into the matter, and among those called to give evidence was the renowned biologist Thomas Huxley. He argued that the Embankment was a better site from the point of view of working class visitors, and quoted an artisan who had declared that the museum 'might as well be in New Zealand as South Kensington for our purpose, because we cannot get there'. Huxley then attacked, as he had done on previous occasions, the whole basis of Owen's museum, proposing that alternate galleries should be devoted to public display and to study, thereby halving the amount of material on show – the narrow 'reserve galleries' would be solely for use by visiting scientists and students, providing ample space to study specimens. Display cases would fill the arches dividing these galleries from the public ones, allowing the general public to view the specimens from one side while scientists could access them physically from the other. A cunning system of trap

doors would lead from the reserve galleries to storage areas holding yet more specimens as well as study rooms. There was support for his views on the Committee but the Embankment scheme, which included a whole range of public buildings in addition to a new museum, proved too ambitious for the newly elected Liberal Government and it was dropped. By 1870 Owen's original scheme for a new museum had been reinstated and, with the budget slashed by yet another newly appointed Commissioner of Works, any hope of a riverside museum was dashed for good.

The changes in government, arguments about the alternative site and, crucially, savage cuts in funding kept Waterhouse busy for several years revising his design but, in 1873, he was back at the South Kensington site. He abandoned the Renaissance style of Fowke's original design, replacing it with a Neo-Romanesque building featuring rounded arches and

The Natural History Museum in South Kensington in c. 1881, around the time it first opened to the public.

massive vaulting. He expressed his own approach to decoration as a willingness 'to clothe over practical necessities with such beauty as they were capable of receiving', combining functionality with beauty at every opportunity. But his intentions for the Museum went far beyond this. His building would be illuminated by a richness of ornamentation that perfectly complemented its contents and the philosophy of science itself. One obvious manifestation of this is the terracotta mouldings that appear everywhere both inside and outside the building as statues and reliefs on columns, and above arches, windows and doors. The other is the painted ceilings of the principal public halls.

The foundation stone of the new museum was laid in 1873, and construction went ahead through the rest of the decade, with it finally opening to the public in 1881. Waterhouse had terrible problems trying to cut back his costs from the original budget of £500,000 to a miserable £330,000, which was all that the new Commissioner would allow him. His solution was to build the south front and the core of the building straight away, with the east, west and north galleries being added as and when funds became available. Quite predictably, funds never did become available, or at least not until the 1960s and 1970s, by which time Romanesque wings were quite out of the question.

Easter Monday, 18 April 1881, was the opening day; 'a great day with the young people of the Metropolis' wrote the author of the first leader in *The Times*. Forty thousand visitors were admitted during the first two weeks that the British Museum (Natural History), as it was officially named, was open. Once they had negotiated the steps, and handed in their sticks and umbrellas (a rather curious security measure), they were free to explore the vast building, with over 1.5 kilometre (a mile or so) of wall space and 1.6 hectares (4 acres) of flooring.

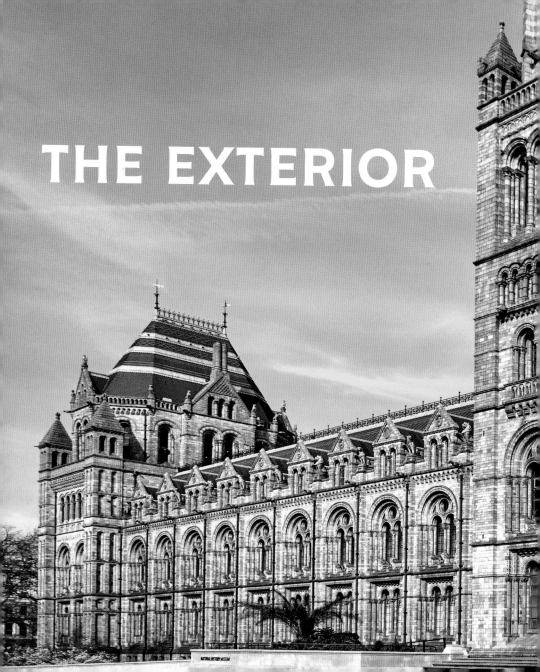

THE EXTERIOR

THE EXTERIOR

THE ALFRED WATERHOUSE PLANS, submitted in 1868, were different to those of Fowke's in many ways, but they were warmly endorsed by the Trustees. The most crucial change was in architectural style. Fowke had produced an Italian Renaissance design, while Waterhouse opted for a round-arched, Romanesque style. Although loosely based on a series of German churches and cathedrals that he had seen on his travels, the new Natural History Museum was no slavish copy of any existing building. Despite its classical basis, the design is clearly and unmistakably Victorian in its use of techniques and materials. In particular, Waterhouse wanted to 'make our buildings effective, even under a gloomy sky', which meant having easily washable surfaces – in this case, terracotta – and soaring skylines adorned with towers, spires and pinnacles.

Waterhouse had to compromise, but one element that was not compromised was his decision to face the building with terracotta. This was a tricky material to use because it was hard to produce evenly in anything but small blocks, and these showed variation in colour. It had already been used on public buildings in South Kensington but only for limited

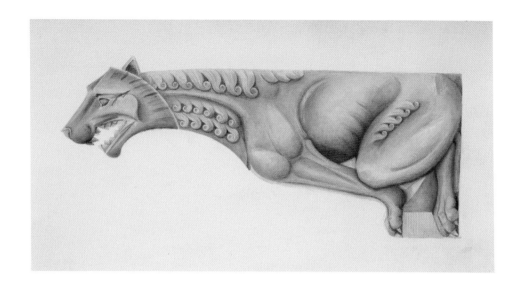

decorative purposes. Waterhouse realised these drawbacks could be turned into benefits and chose to use this material to face the entire building, a first in England and possibly the world. The amount required to clad a structure of this size was so great that the suppliers, Gibbs and Canning of Tamworth, were unable to keep up with demand, a problem that contributed to the bankrupting of the main contractors.

Terracotta retains its fresh colour if washed regularly but this was neglected for many years and the polluted air of London soon turned it grey and dingy, leading to criticism of the architect for choosing so unsuitable a material. However, durable terracotta could also be used in moulds to reproduce an original model cheaply and exactly. This allowed Waterhouse to meet Owen's desire for a building lavishly decorated with natural history motifs. He and Owen worked together to come up with designs for a whole menagerie of animals and enough plants to fill a botanic garden.

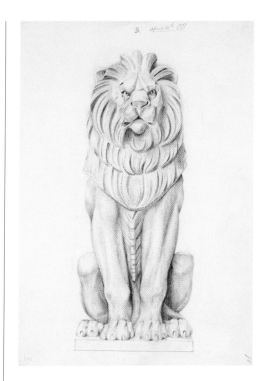

Pencil drawing of a lion, *Panthera leo*. The beast proudly sits on the parapet at the front of the west wing. The species portrayed on the western side of the Museum were, in the main, all extant.

Owen and Waterhouse both thought natural history objects very suitable for architectural ornamentation, and the rich and detailed array of animals that can be found on every part of the building, from parapets and columns to the covers of ventilation ducts, is one of the outstanding features of the Museum. The process for producing the terracotta sculptures was straightforward but exacting. Clay models were made from sketches and the models were encased in plaster to produce a mould that could be used to create the sculptures.

Many hundreds of sketches were produced by Waterhouse himself, although only 135 survive. The sketches are delicate

Pencil drawing of extinct creature *Palaeotherium magnum*. The figure looks out across Cromwell Road from the parapet of the east wing. The species portrayed on the eastern side of the Museum were, in the main, all extinct.

and scientifically accurate and it is suggested that Owen, or perhaps his Keepers, must have provided Waterhouse with specimens or other source materials as inspiration. This must have applied particularly to the extinct animals for which no complete specimens would have been available. As an authority on dinosaurs and other fossil species, Owen's input would have been invaluable. There seems no particular reason behind the choice of subjects and they may simply have been species which one or other man found intriguing for some reason. There was a clear rationale behind the distribution of species around the building. Extinct species were to be

CAPS AT B·B·

ANIMAL AT A

PANELS C

ANOTHER ANIMAL AT A

NEW·NATURAL·HISTORY·MVSEVM· KENSINGTON·

·DETAILS·OF·SOUTH·FRONT·
FIRST·FLOOR·WINDOWS·

bottom line of Cornice

B

B

D

A

C   CAP & SHAFT D

SECTION

PART ELEVATION

SCALE OF FEET

ALFRED WATERHOUSE A·R·A·
ARCHITECT

Photo-Lithographed & Printed by James Akerman, 6, Queen Square, W.C.

confined to the east wing containing the exhibits of rocks and fossils. Extant or living species were to decorate the west wing containing the exhibits of modern zoological species. However, the distinction is blurred, probably by Waterhouse himself. Bats, for example, appear only in the east (extinct) wing despite there being many extant species, while a fossil ammonite appears in the west (living species) wing.

The models were produced by a London-based Frenchman, the sculptor-cum-modeller M. Dujardin. Almost nothing is known of him, not even what the initial M stood for. But clearly he was a talented individual and his skill in interpreting Waterhouse's sketches to produce the master models was crucial. The sketches are two-dimensional and nearly all are drawn from a single perspective rather than the several views usually required. Dujardin had the responsibility or, conversely, the freedom to expand them into three-dimensions in whatever way he chose to interpret them. Waterhouse clearly placed great faith in Dujardin's abilities since the slightest error in the size of the final block would make it impossible to fix it in place. That faith was fully justified and the final products are one of the glories of the museum.

ABOVE The decorative iron gates and railings at the front of the Museum display intricate metal craftsmanship.

OPPOSITE An iron gate pier at the front of the Museum, topped by a gold-plated iron lion.

ABOVE Panels from the stone gate piers at the front of the Museum. From left to right and top to bottom: cobra, *Naja haje*; bird of prey, species not known; pigeon, species not known; orphean warbler, *Sylvia hortensis*; west Indian iguana, *Iguana iguana*; white wagtail, *Motacilla alba*; Senegal bushbaby, *Galago senegalensis*; tufted capuchin, *Cebus apella*; and Eurasian eagle-owl, *Bubo bubo*.

OPPOSITE Stylised snakes.

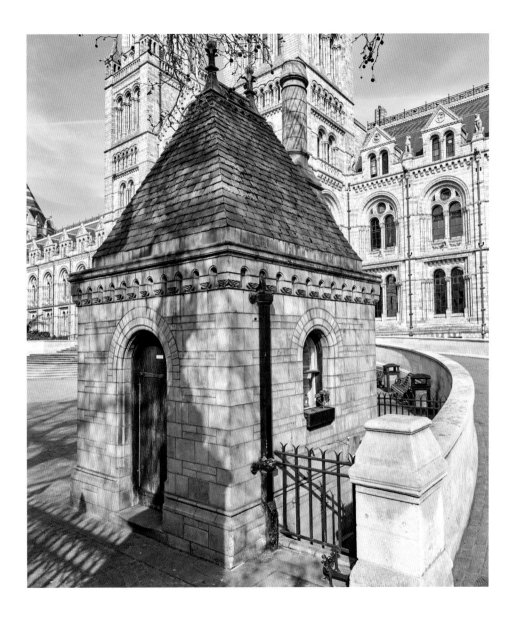

OPPOSITE The remaining porter's lodge (originally there were two), is at the front of the Museum by the entrance gates.

ABOVE A roundel with a lion's head on the rear wall of the porter's lodge.

OVERLEAF Upper part of the eastern roof with extinct creatures.

ABOVE Iron crestings are attached to the main roof. Here, the west wing, bears a kinkajou, *Potos flavus* and Eurasian kestral, *Falco tinnunculus*. In the roundel below, is a wild goat, *Capra hircus aegagrus*.

OPPOSITE Roundels of the dormers on the front parapet. Clockwise from top left: pterosaur and *Palaeotherium magnum* on the east wing; golden eagle, *Aquila chrysaetos* on both the east and west wings; and red fox, *Vulpes vulpes* on the west wing.

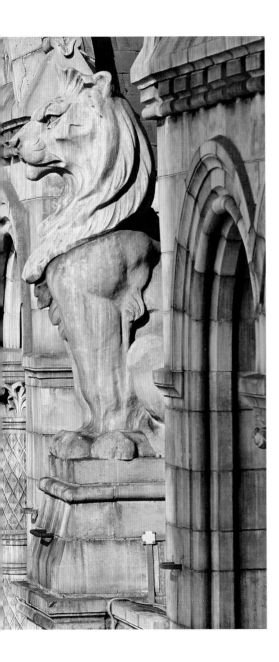

On front of the west wing, three creatures – lion, *Panthera leo;* leopard, *Panthera pardus;* and wolf, *Canis lupus* – stand between the dormers. The grouping is repeated along the parapet, above a row of gargoyles.

ABOVE A *Palaeotherium magnum* (left) and Darwin's ground sloth, *Mylodon darwinii* (right), two of a series running along the parapet of the east wing.

OPPOSITE Lion, *Panthera leo* (left), and leopard, *Panthera pardus* (right), two of a series running along the parapet of the west wing.

Gargoyles below the parapet
on both wings at the front of
the Museum.

OPPOSITE A pterosaur sits at the base of a first floor window on the east wing.

ABOVE Three lion heads adorn the capital for a mullion in a first floor window on the west wing.

OPPOSITE Every part of the Museum is a work of art and the craftmanship on the exterior is a detail often missed in the rush to see the Museum's collections inside. Here, a section of the façade of the west wing.

RIGHT Top: conger eel, *Conger conger* (left); wolf, *Canis lupus* (centre) and unidentified snake (right) and middle: two pairs of scaly dragonfish, *Stomias* sp. either side of a lion, *Panthera leo*. Both are positioned beneath the windows on the first floor of the west wing. Bottom: two extinct fish, lobe-finned fish, *Osteolepis* (left), lungfish, *Dipterus valenciennesi* (right), either side of an extinct mammal are positioned beneath a window on the first floor of the east wing.

A set of three different beasts are repeated along the first floor windows of the east wing: extinct mammal, species not known (above left); sabre-toothed tiger, species not known (left); and pterosaur (opposite).

Three different animals form a set that is repeated along the first floor windows of the west wing: striped hyena, *Hyaena hyaena* (above left); wolf, *Canis lupus* (above right); and lion, *Panthera leo* (opposite).

OPPOSITE The end pavilion of the east wing. The Museum was the first building in England to be faced entirely with terracotta. It was a favoured building material because it could be used to produce cheap durable ornament from moulds that faithfully reproduced the quality of the model from which they were taken. Terracotta is also resistant to acids and easy to wash – it was an ideal material for use in smoggy Victorian London.

RIGHT Dark and light slate roof tiles in geometric patterns are broken up with ruched lead metal work. The ornate iron cresting is completed with a gold-coated fish weathervane.

Two unidentified animals and possibly the golden eagle, *Aquila chrysaetos*, are positioned on the balustrades and gables of the pavilions.

A variety of shells, sea creatures
and insects decorate the mullions
of the basement windows of the
east and west wings.

ABOVE A decorative gold-plated spherical framework of rings, based on an armillary sphere, bedecks the top of both the central towers that stand either side of the principle entrance.

OPPOSITE A set of heads which resemble various wolf-like creatures, dogs and bears peer out from under the small windows of the central towers.

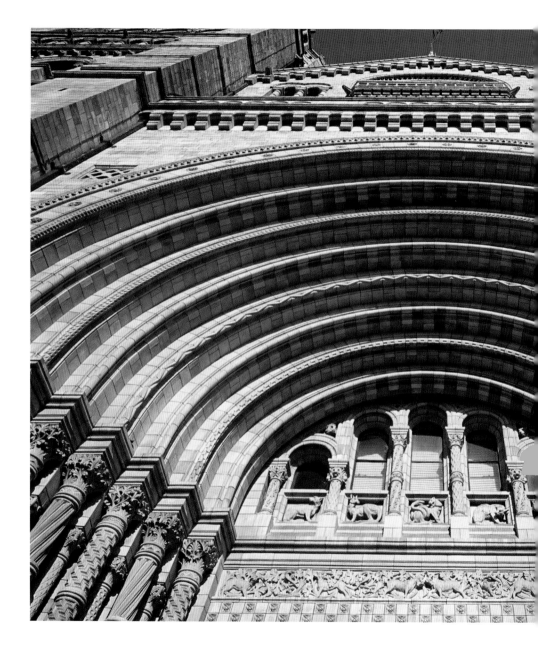

The dramatic arches of the cathedral-like main entrance.

ABOVE Three mythical-looking creatures in foliage are positioned either side of the west wing ground floor windows, by the main entrance.

OPPOSITE Romanesque, Gothic-style patterned shafts stand either side of the principle entrance. Six different designs were produced for the annulets to the shafts and they sweetly break up the repetition of patterns.

Two of four designs that were
produced for the bases of the shafts
either side of the main entrance.

Two of six annulets on the
shafts – possibly a harvest
mouse and frog.

Two cheeky heads peer out from above the windows over the main entrance. They represent an Old World monkey, from the family Cercopithecidae, for evolution and a bulldog, *Canis lupus familiaris*, for Britain.

This set of five panels is above the main entrance doors. A frieze of creatures and foliage runs below the panels.

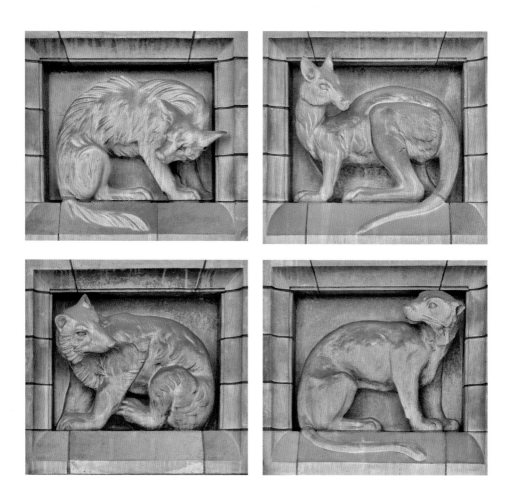

Four of five panels over the main entrance. Clockwise from top left: spotted hyena, *Crocuta crocuta*; Eastern grey kangaroo, *Macropus giganteus*; jaguar, *Panthera onca*; and American black bear, *Ursus americanus*.

The centre panel over the main
entrance doors – a lioness
struggling with an African rock
python, *Python sebae.*

Detail of frieze above main
entrance doors. Birds with nest
and dog, species not known
(above) and goats butting heads,
species not known (opposite).

Capitals next to the doors of the main entrance. Beasts, storks, frog and foliage, species not known (above), and birds and small rodents in foliage, species not known (opposite).

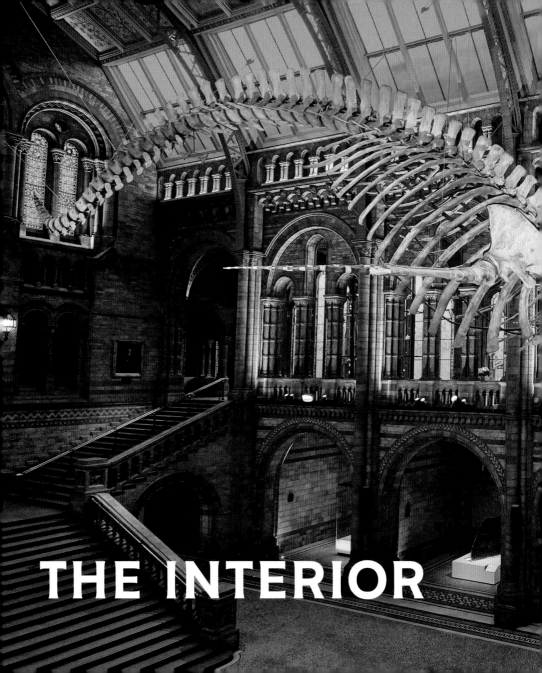

THE INTERIOR

THE INTERIOR

WATERHOUSE'S DESIGN WAS LOOSELY based on a series
of German churches and cathedrals. This is not, perhaps,
surprising given Waterhouse's background and Owen's
expression of the purpose of the Museum, but the
accommodation and inspiration of large numbers of visitors
are also requirements shared by these religious structures.
Certainly the central portion of the Museum has a strong
cathedral-like atmosphere with its nave-like Central Hall (now
Hintze Hall) flanked by pillared galleries and the North Hall
beyond, separated by the grand staircase and coloured with
stained glass. The resemblance is completed by the high,
vaulted and richly adorned ceilings, calling to mind such
Renaissance masterpieces as the Sistine Chapel.

Among the elements Owen wished to include in the new
Museum were an 'epitome of natural history' where selected
specimens would 'convey to the eye, in the easiest way, an
elementary knowledge of Nature'; examples of each 'Class,
Order and Genus' as found among native British species (a
literal manifestation of a 'British Natural History Museum');
and a lecture theatre where Museum staff would give 'short,
elementary, and free Courses of Lectures'. In addition, there

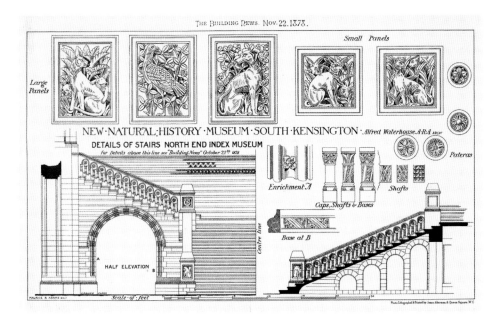

Small Panels

Large Panels

NEW·NATURAL·HISTORY·MUSEUM·SOUTH·KENSINGTON · *Alfred Waterhouse A·R·A* ARCH*

DETAILS OF STAIRS NORTH END INDEX MUSEUM

For Details above this line see "Building News" October 25th 1878

Pateras

Enrichment A

Shafts

Caps, Shafts & Bases

Base at B

Centre line

HALF ELEVATION

Scale of feet

ABOVE Pencil drawing of elements of the interior of the Museum by British architect Maurice Bingham Adams (1849–1933).

PREVIOUS SPREAD The blue whale is the largest animal ever to have lived and the skeleton suspended from the ceiling of Hintze Hall was named Hope to highlight the powerful story it tells about man's relationship with the natural world.

had to be sufficient space to display the largest of specimens, such as whales. Somewhere along the way to a finished building the lecture theatre was mislaid – this facility did not appear until 1947 when the Shell Gallery (now the Jerwood Gallery), which was bombed in 1940, re-opened as a temporary lecture theatre. Today, most interactions between scientists and the public take place outside the original building, in the Darwin Centre. But Waterhouse achieved all of the other ambitious goals by combining these elements of his design with the main routes giving access to the building. Thus, on entering the Museum the visitor was ushered immediately into the Central Hall (now Hintze Hall), containing within its arched alcoves the Index Museum (the 'epitome of natural history') and from which radiated the smaller, more specialised

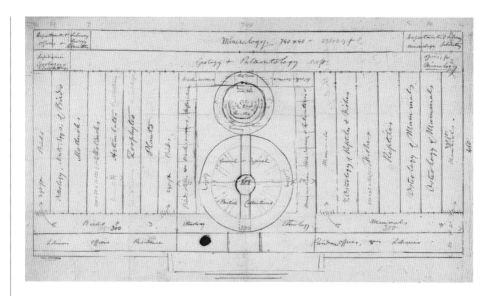

This sketch of the Museum by Richard Owen, made in 1859, shows the layout of his ideal museum, with galleries for different subjects.

galleries; the space was easily large enough to accommodate the largest of specimens. Beyond the grand staircase, the smaller North Hall was for the display of British natural history.

Other major changes to the design were the replacement of the circular Central Hall with a large rectangular one with a smaller hall attached, and the omission of the lecture theatre. The new rectangular halls were to contain the Index Museum, which would serve as a guide to the main exhibits and the British Natural History collections; Owen was determined to retain both of these elements. The lecture theatre had also been a non-negotiable element given Owen's championing of public education and quite why it disappeared is unclear. Owen's unconvincing justification was that the new Central Hall could take on this function, but perhaps he was bowing to pressure from his Keepers who felt they already had sufficient work without any additional responsibility.

The relative contributions of Owen and Waterhouse to the overall design of the building itself are difficult to disentangle, but the concept of a 'cathedral to nature', with a particularly cathedral-like ceiling, clearly indicates they were thinking along the same lines. Richard Owen was a palaeontologist – he was 'the man who discovered dinosaurs' and he was responsible for the division of the ornamentation into extinct animals to the east and living animals to the west that pervades the Museum's external architecture. The ornamentation of the Museum was unusual even for its time, and at its opening in 1881 was thought by some to be 'ornamented – if it may be so termed – both externally and internally with incorrect and grotesque representations of animals, the style of building being more adapted to a suburban tea garden than to a national museum'. It is interesting that attention focused on the animals used to decorate the building – not surprising really, as they were the three-dimensional 'in your face'

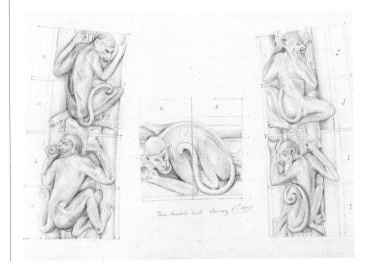

A pencil sketch of a troop of climbing monkeys for the terracotta arches in Hintze Hall,

elements of Waterhouse's design. Animals, and specimens of animals, are three-dimensional and difficult to depict as paintings or two-dimensional images.

The finished models were sent to Gibbs and Canning for production of the final pieces. They were made as oblong panels, roundels, columns, capitals and gargoyles. Some are unique but others are repeated, like the monkeys that cling to the arches of Hintze Hall. The time from completion of the model to delivery of the finished block was eight to ten weeks, leaving no room for error. Given the large numbers produced, simply storing and keeping track of them all was a constant worry for the suppliers.

The sculptures depict a great variety of birds, mammals and reptiles but insects and fish are poorly represented. In all, 97 recognisable species are represented, all of them identified by Waterhouse on his sketches, as well as numerous more generalised items including heads and claws. They include domesticated animals such as the greyhound as well as wild animal species such as a wolf, fennec fox and red fox. Plants, which also cover the painted ceilings of Hintze Hall and North

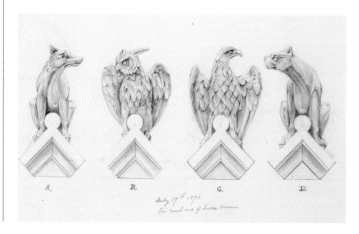

Four fierce looking creatures – two canines, an owl and an eagle – perch astride triangular gablets that are set against the north wall of Hintze Hall.

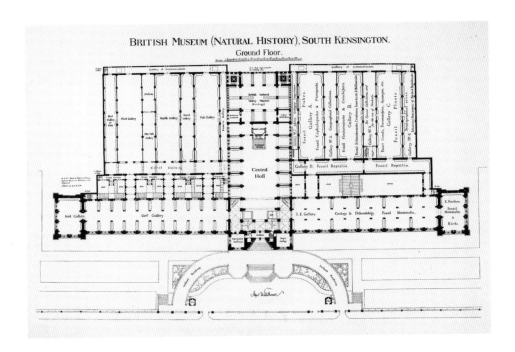

Alfred Waterhouse's 1872 ground floor plan for the new museum.

Hall, appear in terracotta as stems, leaves and rosettes or as panels of decorative foliage. These figures were more than just decoration; they reinforced the educational aspects of the gallery displays. Educational or not, they have delighted visitors ever since.

Waterhouse had to juggle conflicting priorities within his design. In order to accommodate the museum on the site, the main building had to be several storeys high but this caused problems for lighting the exhibits. The smaller galleries running perpendicular to the main building were therefore single-storey, enabling them to be top-lit using only natural light. One flaw was the compartmentalisation of the final building. This suited the Keepers since it was easier for each of them to retain

control over their self-contained departments without interference, but it was certainly hard on the legs of visitors who had to traverse long and convoluted routes. Despite Owen's wish for related departments to be contiguous, anyone wishing to visit both the fish gallery (Department of Zoology) and the fossil fish gallery (Department of Geology) at that time had a walk of 270 metres (295 yards), despite these two areas being only 45 metres (49 yards) apart. It

When Dippy, the Museum's much-loved *Diplodocus* cast, was revealed to the public in 1905 he became an instant star, featuring in news reports and cartoons. He stood in Hintze Hall from 1979 until 2017.

seems odd that Waterhouse, whose architectural reputation derived in part from his ability to effectively direct the flow of people through public buildings, should have failed to provide a more elegant and efficient solution.

The final design of the museum was an amalgamation of ideas – those of Owen, Fowke, Waterhouse and other individuals such as Huxley – and a series of compromises. The ideas were a mix of the traditional and the new, the personal and those more widely held. For example, symmetrical galleries and a grandiose central hall were accepted designs, top-lighting for galleries was a pragmatic approach but the museum also pioneered gaslight to enable evening opening. Building on two levels was a compromise to provide sufficient galleries in the available space. It was also a labour of love for all concerned. In September 1879 Owen wrote 'As my strength fails and I feel the term of my labours drawing nigh, how I long to see the conclusion of their main aim'. The building was completed in the middle of 1880, and the departments of Mineralogy, Botany and Geology were the first to move across from Bloomsbury.

An editorial in the scientific journal *Nature* the following month was, as one might expect, more critical. While admitting that the building was very impressive, the elaborate and ornate internal decoration was condemned as 'a serious mistake', which would impede the layout of displays. The semi-sacred style of the Central Hall was likewise dismissed as 'mistaken', and the writer predicted a perpetual conflict between the views of the Keepers of collections and the architects who built homes for them. Far from being a 'serious mistake', Waterhouse's internal decoration proved to be one of the glories of the building.

Three of four spandrels, which decorate the arches of the vaults in the lobby of the Museum's entrance. Left to right: banded linsang, *Prionodon linsang*; iguana, *Iguana iguana*; common racoon, *Procyon lotor*.

LEFT Some of the many grand arches that show off Waterhouse's complex design and architectural expression. Here, a view towards the east wing from the front of Hintze Hall.

OPPOSITE Hintze Hall is large enough to accommodate the greatest of specimens. In 2017 the Museum's 25.2 metre-long (8 foot) blue whale, *Balaenoptera musculus*, skeleton was suspended from the ceiling.

ABOVE The blue and natural tones of the terracotta decoration complement each other beautifully.

OPPOSITE Unidentified birds in foliage embellish the alcoves of the arches in Hintze Hall. The inclusion of roots could symbolise life and the entire food chain – the plants feed off the Earth and the birds feed off the plant.

OPPOSITE Decorative details on the columns in the entrance lobby of Hintze Hall.

ABOVE A sturdy ram's head looks down from the base of a column on the first-floor balcony of Hintze Hall. In the distance, views of Waterhouse's romantic bridge and secondary staircase are sensational from every angle.

Waterhouse entwined his
animals in foliage, seen here
on the capitals at the top of
columns in Hintze Hall.

A set of six animated heads for the corbels that run along the front of the first-floor balconies in Hintze Hall, pictured together (above) and three in close-up (opposite).

Positioned in a dynamic diving pose, the blue whale, *Balaenoptera musculus*, skeleton is an imposing presence in Waterhouse's cathedralesque hall.

ABOVE The main staircase in Hintze Hall is made of stone and decorated with 12 charming animal panels.

OPPOSITE Two of the smaller panels from the upper levels of the main staircase. Top to bottom: Patagonian mara, *Dolichotis patagonum*, and black grouse, *Tetrao tetrix*, both facing towards the statue of Charles Darwin, one on each side of the stairs.

LEFT Two great cormorants, *Phalacrocorax carbo*, one of the larger panels on the east side ground floor of the main staircase.

OPPOSITE Two of the smaller panels that adorn the upper levels of the main staircase and two of the larger panels for the ground floor. Clockwise from top left: golden pheasant, *Chrysolophus pictus*, on the west side; fennec fox, *Vulpes zerda*, on the east side; red fox, *Vulpes vulpes*, on the west side; and greyhound, *Canis lupus familiaris*, on the east side.

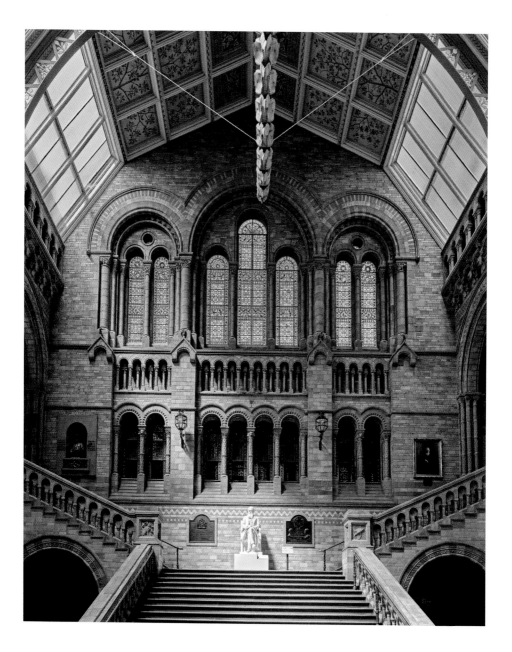

A detail often overlooked, the stained-glass windows at the north end of Hintze Hall bring light into the airy space below.

OPPOSITE In 2008 Charles Darwin's statue was moved centre stage onto the landing of the first flight of the main staircase, facing the entrance, in time for the 200th anniversary of his birth the following year.

ABOVE This view of the upper levels in the North Hall shows a charming combination of cathedral-like columns and arches.

Waterhouse's Romanesque building
features many rounded arches and
patterned pillars, expressing his
willingness to combine functionality
with beauty. Arches and pillars on
the ground floor (above) and first
floor of the North Hall (opposite).

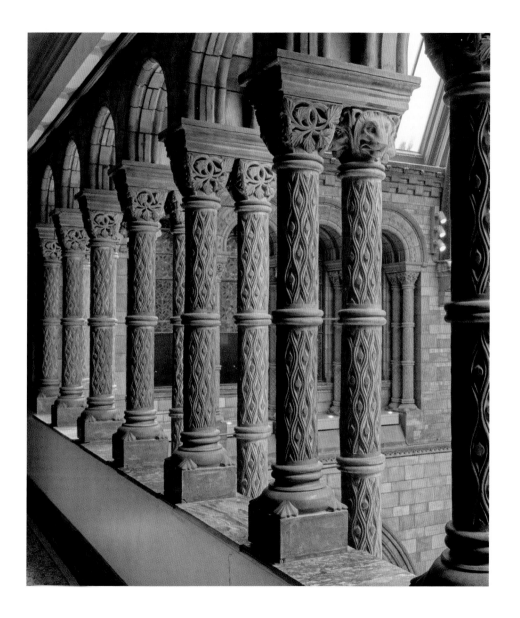

A majestic looking beast looks down from a capital on the first floor of the North Hall.

A view along the western balcony of the first floor (left) and another view looking across from the eastern balcony (opposite).

Foliage and animal figures of perplexed looking canines, ruffs, birds, rodents and other beasts make for dramatic capitals, especially when positioned at the top of intricately detailed columns.

These are positioned at the north end of Hintze Hall on the first floor in the lobbies at either end of the Cadogan Gallery, previously the refreshment rooms.

These large impressive roundels are found above the entrances for the lobbies leading to the Cadogan Gallery at the north end of Hintze Hall: rhea, *Pterocnemia* sp., on the east side (opposite) and pampas deer, *Ozotoceros bezoarticus*, on the west side (above).

A spectacular view from the top landing at the southern end of Hintze Hall. The richness of ornamentation perfectly complements its contents.

LEFT One of the three monkey arches over the staircase above the south landing of Hintze Hall. Each monkey, species not known, is made from two blocks of terracotta with a joint at the waist.

OPPOSITE A tribe of four climbing monkeys. Their cheeky and inquisitive expressions are a fun trait and one that is mirrored throughout the building on numerous other creatures – almost bringing the walls to life.

OPPOSITE The doorway to the south-east gallery on the first floor is protected with ornate ironwork and surrounded by patterns of different coloured terracotta.

ABOVE A dodo, *Raphus cucullatus*, adorns a lunette above a doorway at the far end of the south-east gallery.

LEFT The columns in the south-east galleries are made of iron and support the ceiling. They are clad in ornamental terracotta which protects the iron from fire.

OPPOSITE TOP A pair of capitals showing fossils of ammonites, *Androgynoceras capricornus* (left) and *Crioceratites* sp. (right).

OPPOSITE BOTTOM Vines, flowers and the letters VR (Victoria Regina) decorate the ceilings of the side galleries.

The capitals of the pilasters in
the south-east galleries of the
ground floor, now the Museum
Shop, are decorated with
extinct species in foliage.

Extinct fish and other marine
creatures are positioned on
the lower parts of the pilasters
throughout the ground floor
galleries of the east wing.

A few of the charming details that adorn the arches of the southern ground floor galleries: possibly *Archaeopteryx* (above left) and a pterosaur (above right) in the East Pavilion gallery. Shells and foliage decorate the arches throughout the building (opposite).

A selection of what appear to be sea creatures and an iguana frame the windows in the Museum Shop. It is unclear if these carvings are accurate or stylised by the artist.

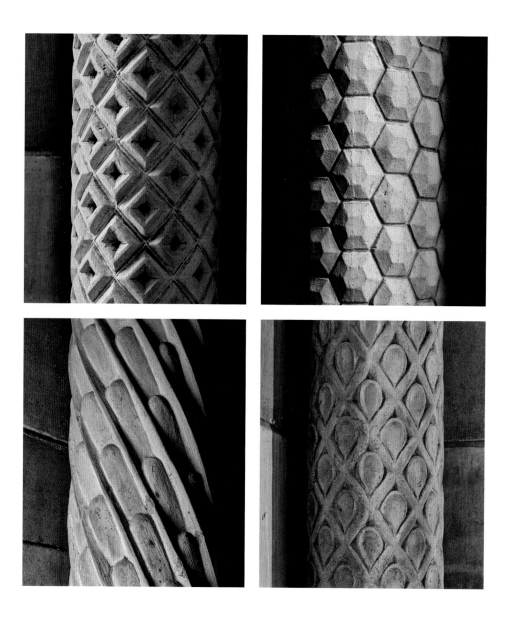

Some of Waterhouse's finer details – four different patterned columns and their decorative bases that can be seen in the southern galleries.

Mice, an owl and a monkey
look down from capitals along
Dinosaur Way.

Simple shapes and patterns of leaves and flowers in muted colours of red, green, yellow and blue are crafted into stained glass windows: north wall of Hintze Hall along the sides of the first-floor balconies (left), at the entrance and exit of the Cadogan Gallery (top opposite) and inside the Cadogan Gallery (bottom opposite).

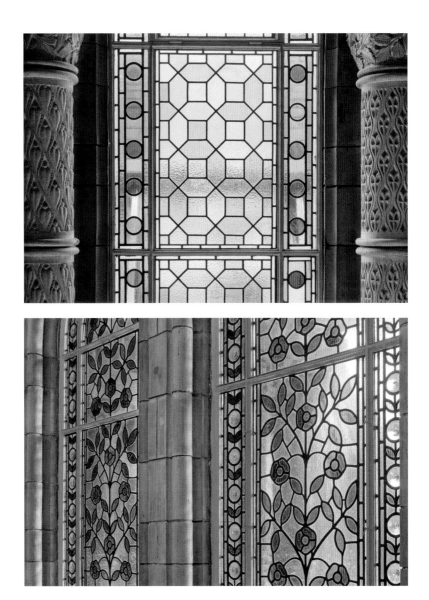

THE CEILING

PINUS SYLVESTRIS

THE CEILING

THE CEILINGS OF THE CENTRAL HALL were to provide a unifying theme but the arrangement and sheer scale of these areas presented a series of design problems. The Central Hall, now named Hintze Hall, was not only large but also very high. Any detail in the decoration of the ceiling was likely to be lost to a viewer on the ground floor. Part of the ceiling was obscured from the main floor area but could be viewed much more closely from the flying staircase leading to the second floor, at the south end of the building. The ceiling of the physically separated North Hall could only be seen directly from within it. Also, Owen took the view that the galleries should be top lit, with light entering from the angle of wall and roof, and Waterhouse carried his idea into the halls. The result was a dark area at the apex of the roof above the skylights. These characteristics meant each area required subtly different treatment while maintaining some kind of consistency of form. The final scheme addressed all of these problems.

The roofs of the halls are mansard types and supported by a framework of wrought iron beams and wooden rafters. Most of the semi-circular main beams or ribs are exposed, but those above the second floor landing of Hintze Hall are

ABOVE Stylised emblems decorate the ceiling of the North Hall amongst the framework of wrought iron beams and wooden rafters.

PREVIOUS SPREAD The plants on the gloriously decorated ceiling panels of Hintze Hall are a mix of native species and those from far-away countries. There are very few records of who painted them and why they were chosen but they are all botanically accurate.

entirely sheathed in terracotta and are invisible. The ceilings are constructed of plaster laid over thin wooden laths nailed to the rafters and built up to form a series of framed panels. Waterhouse's concept for the decoration of the ceilings was explained in an article in *The British Architect and Northern Engineer* magazine from June 1878: 'The lower panels will have representations of foliage treated conventionally. The upper panels will be treated with more variety of colour and the designs will be of an archaic character. The chief idea to be represented is that of growth. The colours will be arranged so that the most brilliant will be near the apex of the roof'.

Although he employed a team of assistants, Waterhouse was intimately involved in every detail of the project. How much assistance he received in selecting the species of plants to be depicted on the ceilings is unknown. Evidence from the scanty documentation surviving suggests that Richard Owen provided specimens for the terracotta models of extinct animals and perhaps had some say in the extant ones too. The man in charge of the Department of Botany, William Carruthers, may have been the source of similar samples for the ceiling and certainly the designs are strongly suggestive of plant specimens as they are preserved in a herbarium. We do know that several of the paintings on the ceiling are based on illustrations in the three volumes that make up *Plantae Asiaticae Rariores, or, Descriptions and figures of a select number of unpublished East Indian Plants,* published 1830–32, by the Danish botanist, Nathaniel Wallich, who was the first curator of the Indian Museum, in Kolkata, West Bengal. Whatever help and advice Waterhouse may have had, the concept of the ceiling and the original sketches were almost certainly his own work, although none of his drawings appear to have survived.

To translate his ideas into reality Waterhouse chose the firm of Best & Lea of John Dalton Street, Manchester. They had already completed a commission for Waterhouse at Pilmore Hall near Darlington and were to work with him on other projects including the magnificent ceilings of Manchester Town Hall and even those at Waterhouse's own home, Yattendon Court in Berkshire. Of the two partners in the firm, it was the artist Charles James Lea who was responsible for the paintings. Lea was asked to 'select and prepare drawings of fruits and flowers most suitable and gild same in the upper panels of the roof'. This implies two things – that Lea made the final selection from a set of sketches provided by Waterhouse, and that Lea scaled up the original sketches to the final panel size in the same way that the sculptor Dujardin scaled up Waterhouse's sketches of animals when preparing the terracotta moulds.

The original allocation for painting the ceilings in colour and gold was £1,800, but spending was being strictly monitored by the First Commissioner of Works (the Minister responsible for public building projects), Acton Smee Ayrton. The First Commissioner, referred to by Sir John Betjeman as 'that stinker Ayrton', despised art, artists and architects, and believed it his duty to curtail their frivolous spending whenever possible. The supposedly extravagant cost of decorated ceiling panels was rejected but, rather than accept plain ceilings, Waterhouse resorted to subterfuge. He argued that the 'application of a

The ceiling panels are in sets of nine, with six of the nine being an individual tree, as illustrated by this Scots pine, *Pinus sylvestris*.

simple decoration in color [sic] will be of a great advantage to the effect of this [the ceiling] and the most important part of the interior of the building'. Furthermore, this could be achieved cheaply if the work were done while the scaffolding used by the main builders George Baker & Son to construct the roof were still in place, thus avoiding the cost of re-hiring it. Quite why Ayrton was taken in by the idea this was a cheaper option than using simple white paint is unclear. Whatever the reason, he missed the chance to shave a few more pounds from the budget and colourful ceilings were reinstated in the design.

At Waterhouse's suggestion, two sample panels, those of the pomegranate and the magnolia (possibly those now above the Landing), were prepared for the First Commissioner's perusal. They must have met with Ayrton's approval since £1,435 was set aside for decorating the ceilings of Hintze Hall and the North Hall. Using the orange and the apple as examples, Waterhouse was also able to persuade Ayrton that the sets of panels depicting growth should be further enriched by the fruits being gilded and glazed in appropriate tones.

The ceilings serve a double aim: they unify the separate halls and at the same time show off nature. Lea would probably have painted the plaster panels in situ, working at the top of the scaffolding like a latter-day Michelangelo. The result is a work of stunning majesty, a gilded canopy soaring above the thousands who walk the halls of this wonderful building. This is where the Museum's design truly resembles that of a cathedral most closely but with a special difference, that of nature itself.

The names of the plants on the ceiling are in Latin, scientific names rather than the common names, reflecting Owen's desire for the new Museum building to be a place for learning including learning the universal scientific names for plants and animals. Common names were fine for general use, but the 'proper use of names' was important for the study of a universal natural history, one that had global application.

The panels in Hintze Hall are arranged in sets of nine, each set separated by giant iron girders that themselves are ornamented with a botanical theme. The naked girders are blatantly strong, supportive metalwork – the skeleton of the building exposed. From the ground they seem to disappear into the rich ornamentation of the rest of the design, but from the landing they look exposed and somewhat out of place amidst the rich earth tones of the rest of the ceiling, almost as if they were put in later, a sort of supportive afterthought. But they are part of the original design. The semi-circular girders referred to by Waterhouse as the 'round-arched style so common in

Southern Germany in the late 12th century' are braced with a decorative zigzag of triangles whose alternate spaces are filled with golden designs that are leaf-like, but highly stylistic and repetitive. The six designs in the bracing repeat from right to left and back again along successive girders, beginning at the southern end of the hall.

Parallel to the lowest burgundy beam and between each row of panels are two additional beams, each with a geometrical design in green and cream rectangles. These designs are simpler than many of the other geometric designs in the ceiling and much less ornamented with gold leaf. This allows the viewer's eye to move almost without noticing it through the panels that make up each individual plant – despite being a border, the geometric design is a unifying feature. Flanking each set of nine panels, almost tucked alongside the iron girders, are frames of abstract leaves, leaflets or perhaps fern fronds. These carry on down to frame the windows as well, providing a link between the solidity of the terracotta walls, the transparent windows and the light and airy ceiling.

The plants depicted in the main hall are a mixture of the familiar, like the English or pedunculate oak, *Quercus robur* and the exotic like chocolate, *Theobroma cacao*. The main pictorial elements of sets of six panels, each with a single named species, are light in comparison with the darker terracotta of the building; the cream background focusing the viewer's attention on the plant itself. Each panel is the same basic design – a central branch arising from the centre panel and dividing neatly into smaller branches into the other five. Looking at the panels, the eye is drawn upwards by the branches themselves; the plants seem to be growing from panel to panel. This device introduces the three-dimensional concept of growth into what is a two-dimensional medium and allowed the artist and architect to depict the plants from close-up rather than as huge, faraway canopy trees. In a way the panels make one feel as if you are in the canopy of a large tree, looking at the outermost branches. Most of the plants in these six-piece sets of panels are trees, and most are either European in origin or were useful to people in Europe at the time the Museum was built. That trees feature strongly in this architectural design seems entirely appropriate. Standing among woodland giants brings a sense of humility and wonder in nature, in keeping with Owen's aims for the Museum.

The plants depicted on the ceiling above the staircase at the southern end of Hintze Hall are a nod to the days of the British Empire and its associated social cost. As a visitor ascended the staircases to reach the upper floors of the Museum, they would have gone south to north, then north to south again. Going up the arched stairway over the entrance, a visitor enters a new, somewhat more intimate and enclosed space compared to the vast cavernous space of the main hall. In contrast with the ornamental iron girders of the open spaces of the main hall, terracotta facings over the structural girders give the portion of the ceiling above the Landing a completely different feel.

Although the apex of the ceiling is a continuous series of panels from one end of the building to another, the panels are different, both in botanical and design – they are individual plants, each labelled with their scientific name. The images are, in a way, designed to be seen from closer to – they do not create a sense of vastness but instead invite detailed investigation, panel by panel. Each panel is of a particular species, each of which has had some influence on human civilisation or trade, and most of the plants depicted are those upon which the mercantilist Empire was built such as cotton, tea and tobacco. When the Museum was being built in the late 19th century, the cotton trade was huge and one of the mainstays of British trading dominance and which stretched across all continents, and the plants in the ceiling come from all over the world. The role of cotton in commerce and trade, and its terrible cost, was sure to have been a topic

Sir Hans Sloane, shown at the age of 76. His personal collections formed the basis of the Museum's collections.

of discussion in abolitionist circles in Britain, and Alfred Waterhouse, as a Quaker, was certainly a participant in such exchanges. It is no surprise then that a plant of such enormous commercial and social significance to the Britons of the mid-19th century should be in prominent display on the ceiling of the new Museum.

Moving from Hintze Hall via archways under the main staircase the focus of the plants changes to the British Isles, with 36 panels in rich greens, golds and reds surrounded by geometric borders. The panels are decorated with plants known from Britain at the time the Museum was built, and this is also the only place in which silvergilt appears.

Although most of the main panels depicted on the ceiling of the great vault of Hintze Hall would have been relatively familiar to most Victorian visitors, two stand out as oddities. Among the British trees, the fruits and the Biblical plants are panels of cacao, *Theobroma cacao,* and showy banksia, *Banksia speciosa*, that really don't fit. But they do have significance to the Museum. The cacao was perhaps in recognition of Sir Hans Sloane who orchestrated the assembling of a natural history collection of specimens that formed the beginnings of the Museum and was credited with introducing cacao to Britain from Jamaica, by way of a bitter chocolate drink. And *Banksia* was named in recognition of Sir Joseph Banks whose endeavours, with the help of artists and other collectors, contributed specimens that form a key element of the Museum's collections.

The arched canopy has 162 illustrated panels showing plants from across the world. It is made of plaster laid over thin wooden laths nailed to wooden rafters and supported by a framework of wrought iron beams. Arranged in sets of nine, the illustrations encompass the familiar and the exotic. The groups of panels are separated by giant exposed iron girders embellished with golden botanical motifs. Three terracotta-clad arches with chains of monkeys separate the panels on the south landing. The apex of the ceiling is lined with 54 panels with blue-green backgrounds. Many of the plants have medicinal uses, while others are purely ornamental. Some, like cotton and tobacco, were plants that fuelled the British Empire's economy.

OPPOSITE The ceilings have survived a variety of damaging events. This pomegranate, *Punica granatum*, from the Mediterranean has a crack in its panel. The panels can be affected by damp, causing the paint to peel. Amazingly, none of the panels were destroyed during the bombing of London in the 1940s.

ABOVE Vegetable ivory palm, *Phytelephas* sp. (left), from tropical America and pepper, *Piper* cf. *ribesioides* (right), from Asia. The flowers of the pepper were painted without knowledge of what they actually looked like.

OVERLEAF Clockwise from top left: arum lily, *Zantedeschia aethiopica*, from South Africa; pineapple, *Ananas comosus*, from tropical America; orchid, *Dendrobium densiflorum*, from Asia; aloes, *Aloe* sp., native range not known; and *Coralluma* sp. from Asia (opposite page).

OPPOSITE *Aristolochia* sp. native range not known.

ABOVE *Viburnum* sp. (left) native range not known and hollyhock, *Althaea rosea* (right), from Europe.

A quintessentially British tree, the English oak, *Quercus robur*, from Europe is most likely featured because of its majestic grandeur and its historic and frequent use as a tough and durable building material. There are 12 trees depicted in all, running from the north to the south end of Hintze Hall, up to the terracotta monkey arches. Each has a set of six interconnected panels, with the branches spreading upwards across the panels from a central trunk.

Lemon, *Citrus limon*, from Southeast Asia is valued for its fragrance and the taste of its fruit. Global exploration had a major impact on British culture and new plants poured into the country during the 19th century as explorers sent home seeds and cuttings. Their discoveries inspired Victorian gardeners to cultivate fruit and flowers from around the world.

THEOBROMA·CACAO

The inclusion of cacao or chocolate, *Theobroma cacao*, from tropical America is perhaps in recognition of Sir Hans Sloane, a London society physician, whose extensive collection of objects formed the seed of the British Museum, of which the Natural History Museum was once a part. Sloane is also famous for introducing drinking chocolate to Britain. He added milk and sugar to a bitter chocolate drink he encountered in Jamaica, which became, at the time, a cure-all for many human ills.

Grape, *Vitis vinifera*, from Eurasia.
In the panels, as in life, each bunch
of grapes and their tendrils differ.
Wine and raisins were common
imports in Victorian Britain.

The bitter Seville orange, *Citrus aurantium*, did not generally grow in Britain, but would have been familiar to Museum visitors as it was a key ingredient in the much-loved marmalade.

A sumptuous combination of colours, patterns and elaborate detail adorn the ceiling over the south landing of Hintze Hall. Each panel is of a separate species and together they tell the story of many of the plants encountered and collected by explorers from all the corners of the known world.

·CASSIA · FISTVLA·

LEFT Canafistula or golden shower, *Cassia fistula*, from Asia.

OPPOSITE Clockwise from top left: holly, *Ilex aquifolium*, from Europe; *Dillenia aurea* from Asia; big-leaf magnolia, *Magnolia fraseri*, from the Americas; and bitter aloes, *Aloe succotrina*, from Africa.

·ILEX·AQVIFOLIVM·

·DILLENIA·ORNATA·

·ALOE·SVCCOTRINA·

MAGNOLIA·AVRICVLATA

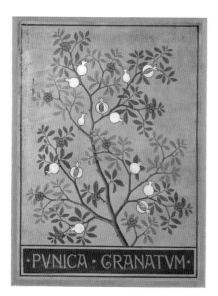

·PVNICA · GRANATVM·

❖ COFFEA·ARABICA ❖

· PYRVS · COMMVNIS ·

❖ CAMELLIA·THEA ❖

OPPOSITE Clockwise from top left: pomegranate, *Punica granatum*, from Europe; coffee, *Coffea arabica*, from Africa; tea, *Camellia sinensis*, from Asia; and pear, *Pyrus communis*, from Europe.

RIGHT Maize or corn, *Zea mays*, from Mexico.

ZEA · MAYS

ÆSCVLVS·HIPPOCASTANVM

OPPOSITE Horse chestnut, *Aesculus hippocastanum*, from Europe.

ABOVE Clockwise from top left: castor bean, *Ricinus communis*, from Africa; bergamot orange, *Citrus aurantium* subsp. *bergamia*, from Asia; dogwood, *Cornus capitata*, from Asia; rhododendron, *Rhododendron formosum*, from Asia; ackee, *Blighia sapida*, from Africa; and sea cotton, *Gossypium barbadense*, from the Americas.

LEFT Hintze Hall leads to the North Hall via archways under the main staircase. Here the focus is on the British Isles, with 36 panels in rich greens, golds and reds surrounded by geometric borders. The uppermost panels are decorated with a central botanical emblem – the thistle of Scotland, the rose of England and the shamrock of Ireland. The lower panels represent plants known from Britain at the time the Museum was built. This is also the only place in which silver-gilt appears.

OVERLEAF Yellow horned poppy, *Glaucium flavum* and foxglove, *Digitalis purpurea*, from Europe.

GLAVCIVM · LEVTEVM

DIGITALIS · PVRPVREA

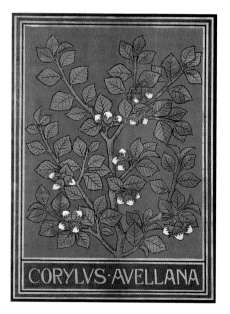

CORYLVS·AVELLANA

SONCHVS·PALVSTRIS

MALVA·SYLVESTRIS

DATVRA·STRAMONIVM

OPPOSITE Clockwise from top left: hazel, *Corylus avellana* and marsh sowthistle, *Sonchus palustris*, from Europe; thorn-apple or jimson weed, *Datura stramonium*, from the Americas; and common mallow, *Malva sylvestris*, from Europe.

RIGHT Greater spearwort, *Ranunculus lingua*, from Europe.

RANVNCVLVS · LINGVA ·

LONICERA · PERICLYMENVM

OPPOSITE Honeysuckle, *Lonicera periclymenum*, from Europe.

ABOVE Clockwise from top left: dog rose, *Rosa canina*; monk's hood, *Aconitum napellus*; spurge laurel, *Daphne laureola;* rosebay willowherb, *Chamaenerion angustifolium;* elecampane, *Inula helenium*; and green hellebore, *Helleborus viridis* – all from Europe.

An array of stencils appears tucked away on the ceilings of the first floor balconies of Hintze Hall. The animals and plants are used as a repeated motif along the length of each gallery.

The ceilings of the lobbies at either end of the Cadogon Gallery boast a beautiful display of stencilled flower shapes, birds, dragonflies, butterflies and bees. These stencils are repeated in gilt in the panels themselves.

ACKNOWLEDGEMENTS

Thanks to the Natural History Museum science department who helped with the identifications to Waterhouse's stylised terracotta flora and fauna interpretations – not all were obvious, so not all images have been described to species level. And thanks to the Museum's photographic unit for solutions to some challenging photography and patience with the British weather.

Text about the history and architecture of the Museum building has been drawn from *Nature's Treasurehouse* by John Thackray and Bob Press with additional information on the ceiling from *The Gilded Canopy* by Sandra Knapp and Bob Press.

First published by the Natural History Museum,
Cromwell Road, London SW7 5BD

© The Trustees of the Natural History Museum, London, 2020

ISBN 978 0 565 09483 6

A catalogue record for this book is available from the British Library

10 9 8 7 6 5 4 3 2 1

Designed by Ocky Murray

Reproduction by Saxon Digital Services, Norfolk

Printed by Toppan Leefung Printing Limited

FSC
www.fsc.org
MIX
Paper from
responsible sources
FSC® C104723